SUMMARY of EAT THAT FROG!

21 Great Ways to Stop Procrastinating and Get More Done in Less Time

by Brian Tracy

A FastReads Book Summary with Key Takeaways & Analysis

Copyright © 2016 by FastReads. All rights reserved. This book or parts thereof may not be reproduced in any form, stored in any retrieval system, or transmitted in any form by any means—electronic, mechanical, photocopy, recording, or otherwise—without prior written permission of the publisher, except as provided by United States of America copyright law. This is an unofficial summary

TABLE OF CONTENTS

BOOK OVERVIEW 3
INTRODUCTION 4
1. Set the Table 6
2. Plan Every Day in Advance 7
3. Apply the 80/20 Rule to Everything 8
4. Consider the Consequences 10
5. Practice Creative Procrastination 11
6. Use the ABCDE Method Continually 12
7. Focus on Key Result Areas 13
8. Apply the Rule of Three 14
9. Prepare Thoroughly Before You Begin 15
10. Take it One Oil Barrel at a Time 16
11. Upgrade Your Key Skills 17
12 Leverage Your Special Talents 18
13. Identify Your Key Constraints 18
14. Put the Pressure on Yourself 19
15. Maximize Your Personal Powers 20
16. Motivate Yourself into Action 21
17. Get Out of the Technological Time Sinks 22
18. Slice and Dice the Task 23
19. Create Large Chunks of Time 24
20. Develop a Sense of Urgency 25
21. Single Handle Every Task 26
Conclusion 27

BOOK OVERVIEW

In this book, Brian Tracy helps readers understand the importance of setting clear goals, managing priorities, and beginning each workday with the most important task. He emphasizes that to become effective a person must write clear goals on paper, list all the tasks required to accomplish each goal, and complete these tasks in their order of importance and sequence. The author concedes that everyone procrastinates, but effective people procrastinate only on trivial tasks. The ability to eat the ugliest frogs first (the most important tasks) is the mark of a high performer.

The book is the culmination of the author's personal experiences, as well as a collection of productivity hacks from influential authors in time management and personal development. It contains 21 practical suggestions that anyone can use to increase personal effectiveness and overcome procrastination. The author has applied these strategies to turn himself from a high school dropout to one of the leading personal development authors.

INTRODUCTION

Today, more than ever, the world faces the unprecedented crisis of overwhelming opportunities and possibilities. Many people don't get around to accomplishing all they set to do because as they complete one task, new responsibilities come up. In a sense, trying to attend to every option, task or project is like putting an octopus to bed: as soon as you tuck one arm in, two pop out. With so much to be done, the ability to select relevant tasks and complete them swiftly and efficiently is, perhaps, the greatest determinant of success today.

Brian Tracy uses the analogy of the frog to emphasize the importance of setting clear priorities and completing essential (and sometimes undesirable) tasks. He reiterates Mark Twain's philosophy on frog-eating:

- When the first thing you do in the morning is eat a live frog, you master the courage to face the day because that is probably the worst thing you're ever going to do.

- If you must eat a frog, sitting and looking at it for very long will only make the experience worse.

- If you have to eat two frogs, start with the ugliest.

The frog represents important tasks that you are likely to put off until the critical moment. The key is to develop a routine of tackling an important task each morning – before anything else and without stopping to think about it. For competing priorities, it pays to start with the biggest and hardest task and see it through before moving on to other tasks.

Tracy observes that successful people (who are paid more and promoted faster) identify major tasks and work on them steadily until they are complete. The discipline to take action immediately and work with a singleness of purpose enables them to achieve specific results and add to the bottom lines of their organizations. Without proper execution, even the best of plans may not come to fruition.

Success habits such as setting priorities, attending to important tasks, and overcoming procrastination, emerge from physical and mental skills that anyone can develop through practice and repetition. As these skills change into habits, they become effortless. At this level of mastery, the immediate payoffs are apparent. With each important task you complete, your brain releases endorphins that give you a boost of positivity, creativity, and confidence. In turn, developing an addiction to these endorphins enables you to complete more tasks on time and subsequently, develop the propensity for success.

The prerequisites for developing the habits of focus and concentration are three essential qualities:

1. Decision – to make a conscious resolution to concentrate on tasks and see them to completion.

2. Discipline – to practice focus routines and other skills until they become effortless.

3. Determination – to pursue desirable habits until they become part of your personality.

As you develop these habits, it helps to visualize yourself as a focused or action-oriented person. Concentrating on the benefits that come with these traits gives you the motivation to practice and get more done. To a significant extent, the mental pictures you form determine how well you learn new behaviors.

1. SET THE TABLE

Before prioritizing or tackling tasks, define your purpose and clarify what you want to accomplish in the key areas of your life. People who get more work done set clear goals and objectives and stick to them. Many people procrastinate because they are vague about what they intend to do and the order in which they intend to complete tasks.

To increase your chances of success, you must learn to think on paper. People who write down their goals accomplish up to ten times more than those who don't.

Tracy outlines a seven-step formula for setting and achieving goals:

(i) Decide exactly what you would like to achieve. Outline personal goals for yourself or discuss your professional objectives with your superior. This discussion reduces the chances on wasting time on low-value tasks.

(ii) Write down your goals. Writing goals on paper transforms them from abstract ideas to tangible, desirable outcomes.

(iii) Set a deadline for your goal. Definite deadlines and sub-deadlines impart a sense of urgency on a goal and reduce the chances of procrastination.

(iv) Make a list of deliverables. Think of all the activities needed to achieve the goal and write them down. The list sets the stage for a definite schedule.

(v) Organize the list. Decide what you need to complete first and organize the activities on the list by priority and sequence. Make a visual map of the sequence using boxes, lines and arrows to show the relationship between the activities.

(vi) Act immediately. Start acting on the plan right away. The success of your goals hinges on your ability to get something (or anything) done.

(vii) Do something every day. Incorporate the activities on the plan into your daily schedule and work on one each day to advance towards your ultimate goal. Don't stop until you achieve your goal.

The Power of Written Goals

Clear written goals not only motivate you to take action, but also tap into your energy reserves and push you to get things done. To draw the excitement you need to get things rolling, set big clear goals and review them on a daily basis. Make a commitment to tackle the most important task each morning.

To get started:

• Take a sheet of paper and list ten goals you'd like to achieve in a year. Write the goals as if you have already achieved them. Use the present tense.

• Select one goal from the list that is likely to have the greatest effect on your life. Write it on a separate piece of paper, set a deadline, list deliverables, and act on the activities that will help you achieve the goal every day.

2. PLAN EVERY DAY IN ADVANCE

Your chances of overcoming procrastination depend on your ability to think clearly, set goals and take action. Planning breaks down a major goal into specific activities and paints a clear picture of what you need to do now. According to Tracy, the ability to make sound plans is a major determinant of competence. Taking ten minutes to plan your day can save up to 100 minutes that you would waste thinking about what to do next over the course of a day. Essentially, planning enables you to use your physical and mental energy efficiently and subsequently increase your productivity and performance.

Two Extra Hours per Day

You can gain up to two extra hours a day and significantly increase your output by consistently working from a list. The night before a workday, prepare a list of all the things you intend to do the following day. Add any new tasks you need to complete to the list as you go about your day. At the end of the day, move the undone tasks to the following day's list.

Making a list the night before not only gives you a clear roadmap of what to do when you wake up, but it also allows you to come up with creative ideas to execute your tasks before you begin working on them.

Different Lists for Different Purposes

Creating different lists for different purposes ensures that you capture everything that you need to do. At the very least, try to make the following lists:

- A *master list* that captures every task, project or idea that you would like to work on in the foreseeable future. Add items as they come up and sort them later.

- A *monthly list* that contains items that you would like to work on in the month ahead.

- A *weekly list* that contains tasks you need to complete the following week. Take a few hours towards the end of the week to compile this list.

- A *daily list* that contains priority items from the monthly and weekly lists. Cross items from the list as you complete them.

Planning a Project

Before tackling a project of any kind, make a list of every step you need to complete and organize these steps in their order of importance. Make a visual map of the steps (showing their sequence of completion) on a piece of paper and tackle each step at a time. A visual map gives you a sense of control, motivates you to do more, and fosters positive forward momentum that undermines the tendency to procrastinate.

Tracy emphasizes that the 10/90 rule should be the guiding principle of anyone looking to increase productivity;

"...the first 10 percent of time that you spend planning and organizing your work before you begin will save as much as 90 percent of the time in getting the job done once you get started."

Key Takeaways

- Always work from a list.

- Plan for each month, week and day in advance by making lists of tasks that you need to complete in each of these periods.

- Sort goals, projects or tasks in their order of importance and sequence. Make a visual map that enables you to see each step involved in the completion of a goal or project.

3. APPLY THE 80/20 RULE TO EVERYTHING

The 80/20 rule holds that 20 percent of your activities, tasks or services account for 80 percent of your results. In a list of ten tasks, two of the most vital tasks will contribute five to ten times the value that the remaining tasks contribute cumulatively. Interestingly, each of the ten tasks may require the same time and effort to complete. In most cases, one task is usually of more value than the other nine tasks put together. This is the task you must complete first. Unfortunately, most people procrastinate on the few vital tasks and spend their productive hours tackling the trivial tasks.

Focus on Activities, not Accomplishments

According to Tracy, people may seem to be busy all day but accomplish very little because they focus on tasks of low value and procrastinate on one or two important tasks that can dramatically improve their results. Understandably, the few valuable tasks are usually the most difficult. Still, you must complete these tasks before tackling the bottom 80 percent because they make all the difference on your personal and professional goals.

Before you work on a task, ask yourself if it is in the top 20 percent or the bottom 80 percent. It is important to understand that starting a workday with the bottom 80 percent activities becomes a habit that is often difficult to break.

Motivate Yourself

You can motivate yourself to work on hard and complex projects by thinking about starting and finishing them. When tempted to complete trivial projects first, remember that the difficult tasks will take as much time and effort – but with five to ten times the payoff. To become effective, you must discipline yourself to consistently eat the ugliest frog first. In the long run, the ability to prioritize and complete important tasks determines your success at work and in life.

Key Takeaways

- 80 percent of your income, profit or other achievement will come from 20 percent of your activities. Identify these activities from your list of monthly, weekly and daily items and discipline yourself to complete them first.

- Resist the temptation to clear trivial activities first.

4. CONSIDER THE CONSEQUENCES

You can easily ascertain the importance of a task by considering its consequences. Anything that has significant repercussions in the future is important, and any activity with few or no long-term consequences is trivial. Having a clear picture of the future enables you to differentiate between important and non-important activities.

According to Tracy, the ability to visualize long-term perspectives of activities and their consequences is a better predictor of success than education, intelligence or connections. Effective people have a clear time horizon that enables them to think up to twenty years into the future. Orientation towards the future forces these people to analyze their present activities and, subsequently, determine if they are in line with their long-term aspirations. Having a clear picture of the future enables you to make better decisions in the short term.

Think about the Long Term

To become successful, you must discipline yourself to delay immediate gratification so that you can reap greater rewards in the future. Making sacrifices in the short-term, such as getting to work early and taking courses to improve your core skills, will have a positive and significant impact on your future. If the potential consequences of completing or failing to complete a task are enormous, make a commitment to start working on it right away.

Obey the Law of Forced Efficiency

According to the law of forced efficiency, there is never enough time to complete every task, but there is always enough time to complete the most important tasks. Tasks and responsibilities will always keep piling up. The best that you can do is take charge of the most important tasks and leave the trivial tasks for later.

Deadlines Are an Excuse

Current research indicates that the pressure of deadlines undermines efficiency because it creates a stressful environment where people make mistakes that result in financial losses. Rushing to complete a task at the last minute often takes longer than expected because rushed activities are prone to mistakes that people have to rectify. Planning and completing tasks in advance offsets the effects of unexpected delays and enables a person to do a better job in a relaxed environment. To make effective work plans, estimate the time it will take to complete a project and add 20 percent more time to the schedule to make some leeway for unexpected events.

Three Questions for Maximum Productivity

To maintain focus and complete important tasks on time, use the following questions as guiding principles. Ask yourself these questions regularly and find specific answers.

• What activities, when completed, will have the greatest impact on your work and life?

• What can you (through your efforts alone) do to make a real difference?

• What would be the most valuable use of your time at this moment?

Key Takeaways

• There's no motivation without motive. Define your future, analyze your choices, and pursue only those activities that bring you closer to your future.

• Base your priorities on the long-term consequences of the actions you want to pursue.

• There's never enough time to complete every task. Focus only on the activities that, if done well, can make all the difference.

5. PRACTICE CREATIVE PROCRASTINATION

Competing priorities and limited time mean one thing: everyone is bound to procrastinate on something. Essentially, the difference between people who are effective and those who are not comes down to what they procrastinate on. To become a high performer, start a workday with the biggest and most complex activities and put off small tasks for later. Alternatively, you can delegate, outsource or do away with low-value activities to focus on tasks that make a difference. Develop the habit of saying no clearly and politely to shut out low-value activities.

Procrastinate on Purpose

Most people procrastinate on important tasks because they don't do it consciously. Purposefully procrastinating on low-value tasks creates time to work on projects that can have a significant impact on your life. To procrastinate on purpose, make a habit of reviewing tasks and responsibilities and dropping those that add little value to your life or work. Cut down on time-consuming activities such as watching television and cultivate a productive mindset every day.

Key Takeaways

• Everyone procrastinates. Successful people procrastinate on small tasks.

• Discontinue low-value activities to get back your time and life.

6. USE THE ABCDE METHOD CONTINUALLY

The ABCDE method is a simple and effective way for setting priorities. To use the method, start by listing all the activities that you have lined up for the coming workday, and place one of the five letters next to each item on the list.

• An "A" item is a very important task that you must complete. Completing or failing to complete this task has serious consequences. If there is more than one "A" item, use the labels "A-1", "A-2" and so on.

• A "B" item is a task you *should* do, failure to which there will be mild consequences. B tasks include returning important calls or reviewing email messages.

• A C item is a task that would be nice to do. There are no consequences for doing or failing to do it. C tasks include calling friends or having lunch with coworkers.

• A D item is a task you can easily delegate.

• An E item is a task you can eliminate with zero consequences.

After making the list, discipline yourself to work on "A" items immediately and persist until you complete them. After that, you can work through the other items in their order. Delegate everything you can and eliminate E items to free up time for important tasks.

Key Takeaways

• Review your daily list and mark each item with an A, B, C, D or E. Start working on "A" tasks and resist the temptation to do anything else until they are complete.

• Set priorities consciously each day to develop successful habits.

7. FOCUS ON KEY RESULT AREAS

A key result area is a responsibility or task that only you can complete. In the workplace, your key result areas provide the inputs that other employees need to complete their work. In management, key result areas include planning, supervising and reporting. In sales, these areas include building rapport, closing sales and obtaining referrals. To become a high performer, identify your key output responsibilities, discuss them with your superior, and ensure your daily activities are aligned with these responsibilities.

Give Yourself a Grade

After identifying your key result areas, grade your performance in each of these areas on a scale of one to ten. Your weakest result area often undermines the outcomes of the other areas and becomes a source of frustration. Instead of avoiding areas of poor performance, set plans to improve the skills needed in these areas. Avoid the urge to rationalize or defend weaknesses. One of the fastest ways to overcome procrastination is to become a high performer in your key result areas.

To increase your effectiveness, identify one skill that, when developed and mastered, will have the greatest impact on your career and life. If you can't identify this skill, ask your superior at work, colleagues, family or friends.

Key Takeaways

• Always ask yourself why you are on the payroll. Your performance on key result areas determines your pay and promotability.

• Identify areas of weakness and set improvement goals. Poor performance in one key result area may undermine the results you achieve in five result areas.

8. APPLY THE RULE OF THREE

Most of the value you contribute to your business comes from three major tasks. Identify these tasks and focus on them to improve your performance. To get started;

• Make a list of all the activities you do in a month or week.

• Ask yourself: If you were to work on just one activity, which one would add the most value to your business?

• Identify the second activity that would contribute the most value to your results.

• Identify the third most valuable task.

Up to 90 percent of the value you add to your organization comes from these three key tasks. Everything else supports these tasks and can be delegated or eliminated.

The Quick List Method

The quick list method can also help you identify areas that you can improve on in your work or life. In thirty seconds, list your three most important life goals. The goals may touch on your finances, career, health or personal relationships. Grade yourself on each goal to identify areas that need improvement.

Expand the exercise and list your three most important goals in your career, relationships, health and finances. Include the three biggest concerns or problems you are facing right now. The answers will reveal what is really important in your life, and where you should focus your energies.

Time Management as a Means to an End

The main objective of developing time management skills is to complete work quickly and free time for personal aspirations. Tracy asserts that as much as 85 percent of people's happiness comes from their relationships with the people close to them. At work, it is the quality of time that matters. At home, the quantity of time spent with your family or friends matters more than the quality.

Balance is not Optional

To strike a balance between work and personal life, make a resolution to utilize all of the time you have at the office. Start with important tasks and resolve to complete as much work as possible. If you don't set priorities and complete your work during working hours, you will inevitably take time away from your personal relationships. It is important to constantly remind yourself that you are working to improve the quality of your life at home.

Key Takeaways

• Determine your three most important tasks and concentrate on them throughout the day.

• Delegate, outsource of eliminate complementary tasks.

• Most of your happiness will come from the personal relationships you have with the people closest to you. Striking a work-life balance is not optional.

9. PREPARE THOROUGHLY BEFORE YOU BEGIN

You can overcome the tendency to procrastinate by ensuring that you have all the materials you need to complete a task before you begin working on it. Start by clearing your workstation to make it conducive for working, and gathering all the information required to complete the task. Ensure your back feels comfortable against your chair and your feet rest flat on the floor. Most activities go uncompleted because people fail to take the time to prepare adequately in advance.

Take the First Step

Begin working on your most important task immediately once you finish your preparations. Focus on getting about 80 percent of the job right because it won't be perfect the first few times. Be conscious of your fears (especially the fear of failure and rejection) as these are the greatest enemies of success. Tracy reiterates that the only way to overcome fear is to immerse yourself in the things you fear most. Master the courage to take the first step, assume the mannerisms of a high performer, and everything else will follow.

Key Takeaways

• The neatness and cleanliness of your work environment determines your level of confidence, positivity and productivity.

• Ensure you have all the materials and information you need before tackling a task.

10. TAKE IT ONE OIL BARREL AT A TIME

One of the easiest ways to overcome procrastination is to focus on the individual actions needed to complete a task rather than on the task as a whole. Work on the steps you can see and you will get far enough as you go. When working on huge projects, take a leap of faith and tackle the first task immediately. You have to believe that the next steps will become clear as you progress. People build great careers and achieve mammoth life goals by completing one small task at a time.

Key Takeaways

• You can overcome procrastination by breaking goals or projects into a list of small steps and working on each step at a time.

• You don't have to have a clear picture of the complete project to begin. Take the first step and the other steps will appear as you go.

11. UPGRADE YOUR KEY SKILLS

Most people procrastinate because they feel inadequate or weak in one or several of the areas needed to complete a task. Tracy notes that,

"The better you become at eating a particular type of frog, the more likely you are to just plunge in and get it done."

Work on upgrading your knowledge and skills periodically because these competencies easily become obsolete in a competitive market.

Never Stop Learning

The better you get at performing tasks, the more enthusiastic you become about these items – and the more likely you are to work on them immediately and overcome procrastination. An additional skill or a piece of new information can help you do a job faster and easier. Identify tasks you tackle every week or month and make a plan to improve the skills needed to perform these tasks.

Three Steps to Mastery

1. Read about developments in your field (from books or magazines) at least one hour every day.

2. Take every course or seminar that adds to your key skills, and attend business meetings and conventions to interact with and learn from other professionals.

3. Listen to educational audio programs in the 500-1000 hours you drive to and from work each year.

Key Takeaways

• You become successful by doing more and better work than others expect of you.

• You can learn every skill you need to increase your productivity – if you make learning a priority.

• The more competent you become, the less likely you are to put off tasks for later.

12 LEVERAGE YOUR SPECIAL TALENTS

Everyone has a distinct set of skills and abilities. You can become a vital link in your organization by identifying these talents and committing to improve on them. Examine your abilities once in a while and take note of what you can do better than other people. You increase your earning ability by becoming better at what other people find difficult to do.

Do What You Love to Do

By default, people tend to enjoy tackling tasks that they are good at. If you enjoy certain aspects of your work, you have the potential to excel in these areas. Find out what you enjoy doing and devote your time to mastering it. Consider tasks or responsibilities from which you receive the most commendations. Tap into these areas to increase your success.

Key Takeaways

- Keep asking yourself what you are good at. Your special talents are the key to increasing your earning ability.

- Develop a plan to refine your special talents to stand out from the crowd.

13. IDENTIFY YOUR KEY CONSTRAINTS

There's always a major limiting factor that stands between you and your goal. It is vital to identify this constraint in the initial stages of a project because it can hold you back and render your goal unachievable. To identify the major constraint, find the one factor that determines the pace at which you complete a job. The factor may be a resource you use, a person you must work with, or a personal or organizational weakness.

The 80/20 Rule Applied to Constraints

If you apply the 80/20 rule, you will find that 80 percent of the limiting factors come from your personal abilities, disciplines or competencies, or from your organization. Only 20 percent of the constraints come from the external environment (external partners, governments and other organizations). To find your limiting factors;

- Assess your abilities and habits to determine if there is something within you that is holding you back.

- Make a list of the steps involved in your job and examine these steps to find what holds you back.

- Examine members of your organization to find the weakness that inhibits progress.

Identifying the most important limiting factor is crucial because tackling the wrong constraint may not solve the problem at hand. The nature of the constraint determines the approach you take to eliminate it. Even when you eliminate a major constraint, you are bound to find another limiting factor because bottlenecks are a constant feature of every project. The pace at which you complete projects or achieve goals depends on your speed in identifying and tackling these constraints.

Key Takeaways

- 80 percent of all limiting factors are within your control.

- Start your day by identifying and removing one key constraint. Often, this is the most important task you must complete first.

14. PUT THE PRESSURE ON YOURSELF

Only about 2 percent of the people in the world are leaders. They enjoy this privilege because they can work consistently without supervision and without waiting for someone to motivate them. You can tap into your full potential by pressuring yourself to apply all of your mental and physical energies into your most important tasks. Set high standards for yourself and aspire to be a role model to others. Keep looking for ways to do more and better work. When you push yourself beyond your limit, you get more work done and increase your self-esteem.

Create Imaginary Deadlines

A good way to overcome procrastination is to work as if you only have a day to complete your tasks. To get into this state of mind, you can imagine that you have to leave town tomorrow to attend a workshop or go on a month-long vacation. Ask yourself what you would need to complete before leaving and start working on it.

While successful people pressure themselves to perform at their highest levels, unsuccessful people wait for instructions and supervision from others.

Key Takeaways

• Set real or imaginary deadlines on tasks and work on important items before the deadline passes.

• Only you can motivate yourself to become the person you can be. Develop a habit of pressuring yourself to do more today than you did yesterday.

15. MAXIMIZE YOUR PERSONAL POWERS

Your productivity depends on your level of physical and mental energies. When you eat well and get enough rest, you complete five times as much work as when you are exhausted. To become a great performer, you must maintain high energy levels throughout the day.

Normally, productivity starts to decline after about eight hours of work. Working for more than nine hours produces less output in more time. The quality of work also declines after the ninth hour of working.

Work at Your Own Pace

To increase your productivity, identify specific hours of the day during which you are most productive and use this time to tackle the most important tasks. When you feel tired, take a rest and remind yourself that you have done all you can. Fatigue undermines your energy and enthusiasm and seduces you to procrastinate on tasks altogether. Sleeping for ten straight hours recharges your body and enables you to get more done the following day.

Get Enough Sleep

To fully recharge:

• Make a commitment to turn off television by 10:00 p.m. every night. Go to bed early and sleep in during the weekends.

- Take a full day off each week – perhaps on Saturday or Sunday. Don't do anything that requires you to think too much throughout this day. You can exercise or take part in social activities.

- Go for a vacation or take a few weeks off work to rest.

Guard Your Physical Health

To keep your energy levels up, watch your diet and commit a specific number of hours for exercise each week. For breakfast, take items low in fat and carbohydrates and high in proteins. Fish or chicken with a salad will suffice for lunch. Avoid products with too much sugar, salt or white flour. Set aside 30 minutes for exercise each day. You can walk, swim or play sports during this time.

Key Takeaways

- Get enough rest, eat healthy, and exercise regularly to increase your productivity.

- Work through the time you are most productive and take a rest after eight or nine hours.

- Pick one behavior that can increase your productivity and practice it until it becomes a habit.

16. MOTIVATE YOURSELF INTO ACTION

To become a high performer, you must become your own cheerleader and encourage yourself to perform at your best. To ensure that things that happen around you do not demotivate you, learn to respond positively to people and situations. Develop the mindset of an optimist.

Your self-esteem – the way you see and talk to yourself – influences your level of motivation. To keep your self-esteem up, ensure that all of your inner dialogue takes place in a positive voice. Practice whispering positive affirmations of the person you would like to become until you believe you are that person. In times of fear or doubt, tell yourself that you have it in you to complete the task ahead. No matter what happens, maintain a cheerful attitude and desist from talking about your problems.

Develop a Positive Mental Attitude

Optimism is one of the most significant predictors of personal and professional success. Optimists possess four special behaviors that enable them to become effective in most areas of life:

1. They look for something beneficial in every situation, no matter how bad.

2. They search for valuable lessons in each setback. Optimists believe that challenges are there to teach them something.

3. They actively search for solutions to every problem.

4. They think continually about goals. Optimists focus on the future rather than the past.

Adopting the optimist mindset enables you to become your own source of positivity, motivation and confidence. As you become motivated, you develop an eagerness to begin tackling and finish your important tasks.

Key Takeaways

1. Your thoughts influence your self-esteem and level of motivation. Learn to control them.

2. Keep a positive mind by looking for the good in every situation, searching for areas to make progress in difficult situations, and focusing on your goals.

17. GET OUT OF THE TECHNOLOGICAL TIME SINKS

Although information technologies are vital in easing communication, they come with crippling dangers that, if left unchecked, may leave you psychologically drained. In particular, the compulsion to communicate and consume information all the time leaves little time to meditate. To maintain high levels of energy and remain clearheaded, detach yourself from communication technologies that may trap you in a time sink – especially when away from work.

Technology exists to ease the speed and accuracy of information and, subsequently, enable you to accomplish tasks faster and more efficiently. Technology becomes an addiction when the first thing you do in the morning is check voice mail or email to see if anyone sent you a message while you slept. Checking personal digital assistants and other communication modes every few minutes is a sign that things are getting out of control. If you spend too much time on communication, you risk leaving important tasks undone.

Take Back Your Time

Apply the 80/20 rule to communication: 80 percent of the email messages you receive are of no value and should be discarded. Of the valuable 20 percent, only a few require immediate action. You can concentrate on completing important tasks and respond to these messages later or delegate this task altogether. If there is only enough time to sort emails or perform other important tasks, ignore the messages. If they are important enough, the sender will attempt to reach you again.

Discipline yourself to use technology as an aide rather than an obstacle. Resist the urge to turn on your cellphone, television or radio until you have planned your day. Create silence zones that bring out your inner creative genius. Remind yourself that even when you get away from work for a day or month, other people keep things moving. If something important happens, someone will always finds a way to let you know.

Key Takeaways

• 80 percent of all email messages are low-value items that should go to the bottom of your do-list.

• Discipline yourself to turn off your communication devices at least two hours during the day to take charge of your life and plan for important tasks.

• Detach yourself from communication devices to give your mind time to recharge.

18. SLICE AND DICE THE TASK

Most people procrastinate because they feel that the task at hand is too big to complete. To overcome the feeling of being overwhelmed by a project, dissect it into small deliverables and resolve to complete just one item for the time being. When you complete one item, you are likely to feel like completing another one. Part by part, you will soon find that the project is almost done.

Develop a Compulsion to Closure

Psychologically, everyone possesses an urge to complete things already in motion. You invite this urge by starting tasks immediately. This urge not only motivates you to begin working on a task you have planned for, but also pushes you towards completion. This compulsion is addictive because completion releases endorphins that make you feel happier and more powerful than before. Every step of a project you complete energizes you and pushes you to completion.

"Swiss Cheese" Your Tasks

Alternatively, you can get things rolling by resolving to use a certain period to punch a hole in a major project. You can decide to use the next five or thirty minutes to do a small part of the project and move on to something else. Once you start working on the task, your compulsion to closure may motivate you to complete a significant chunk of the project.

Key Takeaways

• Break down a major task into small pieces and resolve to complete just one piece.

• Completing a small part of a big project may not seem like much but once you get to it, you develop a forward momentum that pushes you to completion.

• Take action immediately. Staring at a frog you're supposed to eat does not help.

19. CREATE LARGE CHUNKS OF TIME

Important projects often require large amounts of uninterrupted time to complete. To become successful in work and life, you must set aside chunks of high-value time to complete important tasks – especially the ones you don't like. You must have the discipline to see the task to completion without wandering off to other low-value activities.

To set long unbroken sessions, plan your working day in advance and reserve hour-long segments for completing important tasks. Make a commitment to complete these tasks within the preplanned time slots. Use a time planner to organize your workweek by days, hours and minutes. During the time you set for concentrated work, remove all distractions from your workstation – including turning off the phone – and work nonstop. You can get more work done by setting large chunks of time in the morning when there are few distractions.

Make Every Minute Count

Before you fly on business, plan for important tasks and try to accomplish as much as possible during the flight. Airplanes are great places to work in because they have few distractions. Use travel and other transitions times to complete pieces of large projects.

Key Takeaways

• Use a time planner to find periods where you can schedule large chunks of uninterrupted time for important tasks.

• Think creatively to find time to complete pieces of large projects. Make every minute count.

20. DEVELOP A SENSE OF URGENCY

You can identify high-performing people by their desire to complete tasks as soon as possible. They devote some time to plan and set priorities and take action immediately. By working steadily and continuously, they get more done in less time than the average person. When you work on a task intensely and continuously, you reach a mental state where tasks seem effortless. You experience a sense of calmness, clarity and high competence. When you reach this state, your mind develops insights that enable you to complete tasks faster and more accurately.

You can trigger this state by developing an impatience that compels you to complete tasks quickly. A sense of urgency pushes you to take action immediately and spend minimal time talking about tasks. To develop a high-productivity state of mind, you must start moving now and maintain a steady pace until you complete the job at hand.

Build up a Sense of Momentum

Taking continuous action often triggers the Momentum Principle of success. The principle holds that although it may take a lot of time and energy to start a task, it takes less energy to keep things rolling. The faster you move, the easier it becomes to reach completion. If you find yourself stalling, repeat the phrase "Do it now!" until you get started on a task.

Key Takeaways

• Gather what you have and start where you are. There will never be a perfect time for anything.

• Identify areas where you procrastinate and resolve to take action immediately and move quickly until you get into flow.

21. SINGLE HANDLE EVERY TASK

All the planning and prioritizing you do sets the stage for the most important part: tackling the task. Your success depends on your ability to identify an important task and work on it with a singleness of purpose until you complete it. Single handling a task means working on a task continuously without wading off to do other things.

You can reduce the time it takes to complete a task by up to 50 percent if you resist the temptation to work on anything else until the task is complete. Every time you pick a task from where you left, you have to familiarize yourself with past deliverables and overcome some mental blocks. When you work nonstop, you gain the momentum that enables you to work faster and effectively. When you set your priorities, any activity that does not support the most important task is a waste of your time.

Self-Discipline is the Key

Success in work and life requires mastery, self-discipline, and self-control. To become a high performer, you must force yourself to work on tasks during their designated periods – whether you feel like working on them or not. The more you work on individual tasks until they are 100 percent complete, the easier it becomes to maintain high levels of persistence. Through persistence, you become a master of your destiny.

Key Takeaways

• To become efficient: set priorities, identify the most important task, and begin working on it immediately. Resist the urge to do anything else until the task is 100 percent complete.

• Through constant practice you can learn to work persistently and make progress on the efficiency curve.

CONCLUSION

In essence, the key to personal and professional success lies in the ability to tackle the most important task of the day before doing anything else. Eating the ugliest frog in the morning is a habit that anyone can learn through repetition and persistence. The key is to practice each of the 21 rules for overcoming procrastination until they become engrained in your thought processes and daily routines. When you practice these rules until they become effortless, your potential for success becomes unlimited.

END

If you enjoyed this summary, please leave 5 stars and an honest review on Amazon.com!

Summary of Ego is the Enemy: by Ryan Holiday

Summary of Tribe: by Sebastian Junger

Summary of You Are a Badass: by Jen Sincero

Summary of Grit: by Angela Duckworth

Made in the USA
San Bernardino, CA
26 January 2017